Ready...Set...
Read!

Ready...Set... Read!

THE BEGINNING READER'S TREASURY

Compiled by

JOANNA COLE AND
STEPHANIE CALMENSON

GUILDAMERICA
B O O K S ®

DOUBLEDAY BOOK & MUSIC CLUBS, INC.
GARDEN CITY, NEW YORK

To Karen Stechel

ART DIRECTION BY DIANA KLEMIN

BOOK DESIGN BY DAVID NOVEMBER & CO., INC.

ISBN 1-56865-008-6

ACKNOWLEDGMENTS

We would like to thank Dr. Clinton Hatchett, astronomer at the American Museum of Natural History, for his careful review of *Our Earth in Space.*

"I Had A Dream Last Night" (originally titled "Andre") from BRONZEVILLE BOYS AND GIRLS by Gwendolyn Brooks. Copyright © 1956, renewed 1986 by Gwendolyn Brooks Blakely. Reprinted by permission of Harper & Row, Publishers, Inc.

"The Fat Cat," "Giggle Poem," and *"Seven Sillies in a Row"* by Stephanie Calmenson. Copyright © 1990 by Stephanie Calmenson. Used by permission of the author.

"I Wouldn't" from YOU READ TO ME, I'LL READ TO YOU by John Ciardi. Copyright © 1962. Reprinted by permission of Judith H. Ciardi.

"Our Earth in Space" by Joanna Cole. Copyright © 1990 by Joanna Cole. Used by permission of the author.

"Driving to the Beach" by Joanna Cole. © 1973 by Joanna Cole. Used by permission of the author.

"Fun and Games" selections by Joanna Cole and Stephanie Calmenson. Copyright © 1990 by Joanna Cole and Stephanie Calmenson. Used by permission of the authors.

"Baby Chick" from RUNNY DAYS, SUNNY DAYS by Aileen Fisher. Copyright 1958 by Aileen Fisher, © renewed 1986. Originally published by Abelard-Schuman, N.Y. Used by permission of Aileen Fisher.

"Soft Boiled Egg" from BREAD AND JAM FOR FRANCES by Russell Hoban. Text copyright © 1964 by Russell C. Hoban. Reprinted by permission of Harper & Row, Publishers, Inc.

"I Liked Growing" from DOGS AND DRAGONS, TREES AND DREAMS by Karla Kuskin. Originally published in ANY ME I WANT TO BE by Karla Kuskin. Copyright © 1972 by Karla Kuskin. Reprinted by permission of Harper & Row, Publishers, Inc.

"Ice Cream" from FROG AND TOAD ALL YEAR by Arnold Lobel. Copyright © 1976 by Arnold Lobel. Reprinted by permission of Harper & Row, Publishers, Inc.

CONTENTS

Stories

FROM SHEEP IN A JEEP   12
by Nancy Shaw
Illustrated by Margot Apple

WHAT WILL LITTLE BEAR WEAR?   27
by Else Holmelund Minarik
Illustrated by Maurice Sendak

FROG AND TOAD: ICE CREAM   38
by Arnold Lobel

OUR EARTH IN SPACE   50
by Joanna Cole
Illustrated by Giulio Maestro

MORRIS HAS A COLD   66
by Bernard Wiseman

Poems

Illustrated by Anne Burgess
THE FAT CAT   84
by Stephanie Calmenson
NOTICE   85
by David McCord
HELLO, HELLO   86
by Eve Merriam
BABY CHICK   88
by Aileen Fisher
SEVEN SILLIES IN A ROW   90
by Stephanie Calmenson

GIGGLE POEM   91
    by Stephanie Calmenson

I WOULDN'T   92
    by John Ciardi

I LEFT MY HEAD   94
    by Lilian Moore

I LIKED GROWING   96
    by Karla Kuskin

SOFT-BOILED EGG   98
    by Russell Hoban

EATING WORMS   99
    Traditional Rhyme

TEENY TINY GHOST   100
    by Lilian Moore

I HAD A DREAM LAST NIGHT   102
    by Gwendolyn Brooks

DRIVING TO THE BEACH   104
    by Joanna Cole

AT THE SEA-SIDE   105
    by Robert Louis Stevenson

THIS IS MY ROCK   106
    by David McCord

Fun and Games

by Joanna Cole and Stephanie Calmenson
Illustrated by Chris Demarest

RIDDLES 110

HURRY! HURRY! 122

TONGUE-TWISTERS 124

I LIKE CAKE! 128

DID YOU EVER SEE…? 130

A WHALE TALE 134

FIND THE HIDDEN PICTURES 136

COME TO MY HOUSE 138

Index 142

Stories

SHEEP IN A JEEP
by Nancy Shaw   Illustrated by Margot Apple

Beep! Beep!
Sheep in a jeep
on a hill that's
steep.

Uh-oh!
The jeep won't go.
Sheep leap
to push the jeep.

Sheep shove.
Sheep grunt.

Sheep don't think
to look up front.

Jeep goes splash!
Jeep goes thud!

18

Jeep goes deep
in gooey mud.

Sheep tug.

Sheep shrug.

Sheep yelp.

Sheep get help.

Jeep comes out.

Sheep shout.

Sheep cheer.
Oh, dear!
The driver sheep
forgets to steer.

Jeep in a heap.

Sheep weep.

24

Sheep sweep
the heap.

Jeep for sale — cheap.

What Will Little Bear Wear?

by Else Holmelund Minarik   Illustrated by Maurice Sendak

It is cold.

See the snow.

See the snow come down.

Little Bear said, "Mother Bear,

I am cold.

See the snow.

I want something to put on."

So Mother Bear made something
for Little Bear.

"See, Little Bear," she said,

"I have something for my little bear.

Here it is.

Put it on your head."

"Oh," said Little Bear,

"it is a hat.

Hurray! Now I will not be cold."

Little Bear went out to play.

Here is Little Bear.

"Oh," said Mother Bear,

"do you want something?"

"I am cold," said Little Bear.

"I want something to put on."

So Mother Bear made something

for Little Bear.

"See, Little Bear," she said,

"I have something,

something for my little bear.

Put it on."

"Oh," said Little Bear,

"it is a coat.

Hurray! Now I will not be cold."

Little Bear went out to play.

Here is Little Bear again.

"Oh," said Mother Bear,

"do you want something?"

"I am cold," said Little Bear.

"I want something to put on."

So Mother Bear made something
again for Little Bear.
"See, Little Bear," she said,
"here is something,
something for my little bear.
Now you cannot be cold.
Put it on."

"Oh," said Little Bear,
"snow pants. Hurray!
Now I will not be cold."
Little Bear went out to play.

Here is Little Bear again.

"Oh," said Mother Bear,

"what can you want now?"

"I am cold," said Little Bear.

"I want something to put on."

"My little bear," said Mother Bear,

"you have a hat,

you have a coat,

you have snow pants.

Do you want a fur coat, too?"

"Yes," said Little Bear.

"I want a fur coat, too."

Mother Bear took the hat, the coat,

and the snow pants.

"See," said Mother Bear,

"there is the fur coat."

"Hurray!" said Little Bear.

"Here is my fur coat.

Now I will not be cold."

And he was not cold.

What do you think of that?

One hot summer day

Frog and Toad sat by the pond.

"I wish we had some

sweet, cold ice cream," said Frog.

"What a good idea," said Toad.

"Wait right here, Frog.

I will be back soon."

Toad went to the store.

He bought two big ice-cream cones.

Toad licked one of the cones.

"Frog likes chocolate best,"

said Toad, "and so do I."

Toad walked along the path.

A large, soft drop

of chocolate ice cream

slipped down his arm.

"This ice cream

is melting in the sun,"

said Toad.

Toad walked faster.

Many drops

of melting ice cream

flew through the air.

They fell down on Toad's head.

"I must hurry back

to Frog!" he cried.

More and more

of the ice cream

was melting.

It dripped down

on Toad's jacket.

It splattered

on his pants

and on his feet.

"Where is the path?"

cried Toad.

"I cannot see!"

Frog sat by the pond
waiting for Toad.
A mouse ran by.

"I just saw something awful!"
cried the mouse.
"It was big and brown!"

"Something covered

with sticks and leaves is moving

this way!" cried a squirrel.

"Here comes a thing with horns!"

shouted a rabbit.

"Run for your life!"

"What can it be?" asked Frog.

Frog hid behind a rock.

He saw the thing coming.

It was big and brown.

It was covered

with sticks and leaves.

It had two horns.

"Frog," cried the thing.

"Where are you?"

"Good heavens!"

said Frog.

"That thing is Toad!"

Toad fell into the pond.

He sank to the bottom

and came up again.

"Drat," said Toad.

"All of our sweet, cold ice cream

has washed away."

"Never mind," said Frog.

"I know what we can do."

Frog and Toad quickly ran back

to the store.

Then they sat in the shade

of a large tree

and ate

their chocolate

ice-cream cones

together.

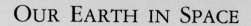

OUR EARTH IN SPACE

by Joanna Cole
Illustrated by Giulio Maestro

Long ago, people thought
the Earth was flat.

"If we walk far enough,
we will fall off,"
they said.

Then some people noticed something.

They saw ships coming

over the sea.

At first, they saw just the tops

of the sails.

Then they saw more of the sails.

At last, they saw the whole ship.

"The Earth must be round,"

thought these people.

Today, we can see
that they were right.
Space ships send back pictures
of our beautiful Earth
floating in space.

We can see blue water.
We can see brown and green land.
We can see fluffy white clouds.
We can see that the Earth is round.

Long ago, people watched the Sun.

They thought the Sun moved.

It seemed to rise in the east.

It seemed to move across the sky.

At night, it sank in the west.

The Earth seemed to stay still.

The Earth seemed much bigger

than the little Sun in the sky.

Earth

Now we know that the Sun

is very big.

It is much, much bigger

than the Earth.

It only looks small to us

because it is so far away.

And we know that the Sun

Sun

does not really move

across the sky.

It is the *Earth* that moves.

The Earth travels around the Sun
and spins slowly like a top.

The side of the Earth
that faces the Sun is light.
The other side is dark.
In this way,
the spinning of the Earth
makes day and night.

Long ago, people watched
the sky at night.
The stars looked like tiny lights.
Today, everyone knows that stars
are not really tiny.
The stars we see are
giant balls of fire.
Our Sun is a star, too.
Many stars are even bigger
than our Sun.
They look smaller because they
are much, much farther away.

In the night sky,

we can see planets, too.

Without a telescope,

the planets look like stars.

But they are really

worlds like the Earth.

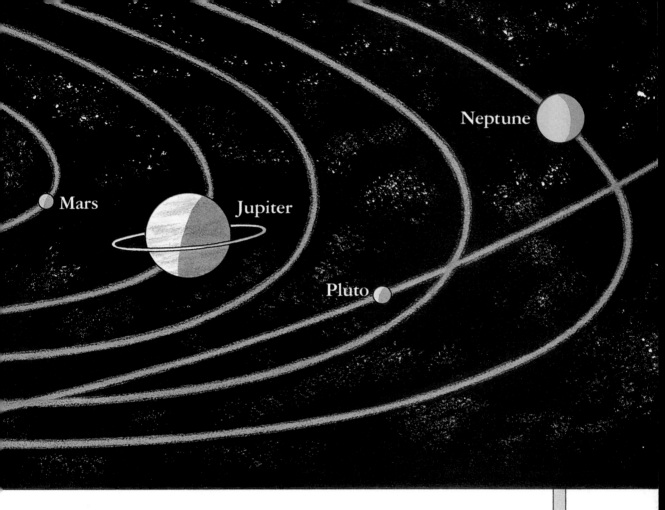

There are nine planets all together—
our Earth and eight others.
In the past, people could only
see planets through a telescope.
Now we send space ships
to visit the planets.

Maybe some day you will visit a planet.

Maybe you will find out something new
about the stars, the Sun or the Moon.

Maybe some day *you* will travel in space!

Morris the Moose said,

"I have a cold.

My nose is walking."

Boris the Bear said,

"You mean

your nose is running."

"No," said Morris.

"My nose is walking.

I only have

a little cold."

Boris said,

"Let me feel your forehead."

Morris said,

"I don't have four heads!"

Boris said,

"I know you don't have four heads.

But this is called your forehead."

Morris said, "That is my ONE head."

"All right," Boris growled.

"Let me feel your one head."

Boris said,

"Your one head feels hot.

That means you are sick.

You need some rest.

You should lie down."

Morris coughed.

Boris asked, "How does
your throat feel?"

Morris said, "Hairy,"

"No, no," said Boris.

"I don't mean outside.

How does it feel INSIDE?"

Morris said, "I will see . . .

"No! No! No!" Boris shouted.

"Ohhh—just open your mouth.

Let me look inside."

"Now stick out your tongue,"
Boris said.

Morris said, "I will not stick out
my tongue. That is not nice."

Boris shouted,

"Stick out your tongue!"

Morris stuck out his tongue.

"STOP!" Boris roared.

"That is not nice!"

Morris said,

"I told you it was not nice."

Boris growled, "That's because

you did it the wrong way.

Look—This is how

to stick out your tongue."

Boris looked at Morris' tongue.

"Your tongue is white.

That means your stomach is upset,"

said Boris.

"Here is a bowl of nice, hot soup.

It will make you feel better,"

said Boris.

Morris licked the soup.

"No," said Boris.

"Use the spoon."

Morris used the spoon.

"No, no," said Boris.

"Put the spoon in your mouth."

Morris put the spoon

in his mouth.

"No! No! No!" Boris shouted.

"Give me the spoon!"

Boris fed Morris the soup.

The next morning Morris said,

"My nose is not walking.

My one head is not hot.

My cold is better.

Make me a big breakfast."

"All right," said Boris.

"But you have to do

something for me . . ."

Morris asked, "What?"

"DON'T EVER GET SICK AGAIN!"

Poems

Illustrated by Anne Burgess

THE FAT CAT
by Stephanie Calmenson

Fat

Fat cat

Fat cat sat

Fat cat sat on ME!

I have a dog.

I had a cat.

I've got a frog

Inside my hat.

HELLO, HELLO
by Eve Merriam

Hello, hello,

who's calling, please?

Mr. Macaroni

and a piece of cheese.

Hello, hello,

hello, who's there?

Honey Buzzbee

and a big brown bear.

Hello, hello,

will you spell your name?

It's R.A.T.

and yours is the same.

Hello, hello,

what did you say?

The rain is over,

let's go out and play.

BABY CHICK
by Aileen Fisher

Peck

   peck

   peck

on the warm brown egg.

OUT comes a neck.

OUT comes a leg.

How

    does

        a chick,

who's not been about,

discover the trick

of how to get out?

SEVEN SILLIES IN A ROW
by Stephanie Calmenson

Seven sillies in a row.

Four named Millie, three named Moe.

Silly shoes, silly hat,

They've even got a silly cat.

Seven sillies in a row.

They show off the things they know.

They think two plus two is three.

That's how silly they can be.

Giggle giggle

Grin grin.

Let it out.

Don't hold it in.

Chuckle chuckle

Tee hee.

Louder now,

Set it free!

Ha-ha,

ha-ha,

ha-ha,

HA!

There's a mouse house

In the hall wall

With a small door

By the hall floor

Where the fat cat

Sits all day,

Sits that way

All day

Every day

92

Just to say,

"Come out and play"

To the nice mice

In the mouse house

In the hall wall

With the small door

By the hall floor.

And do they

Come out and play

When the fat cat

Asks them to?

Well, would you?

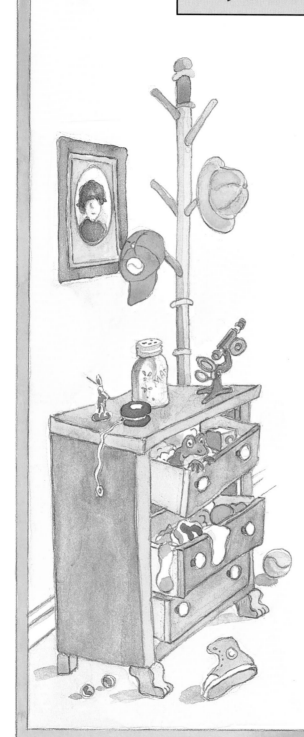

I left my head

somewhere

today.

Put it down for

just

a minute.

Under the table?

On a chair?

Wish I were

able

to say

where.

Everything I need

is

in it!

94

I LIKED GROWING
by Karla Kuskin

I liked growing.

That was nice.

The leaves were soft

The sun was hot.

I was warm and red and round

Then someone dropped me in a pot.

Being a strawberry isn't all pleasing.

This morning they put me in ice cream.

I'm freezing.

SOFT-BOILED EGG
by Russell Hoban

I do not like the way you slide,

I do not like your soft inside,

I do not like you many ways,

And I could do for many days

Without eggs.

EATING WORMS
Traditional Rhyme

Nobody loves me.

Everybody hates me.

I'm going to eat some worms.

Short ones, tall ones,

Fat ones, skinny ones.

I'm going to eat some worms!

TEENY TINY GHOST

by Lilian Moore

A teeny, tiny ghost

no bigger than a mouse,

at most,

lived in a great big house.

It's hard to haunt

a great big house

when you're a teeny tiny ghost

no bigger than a mouse,

at most.

He did what he could do.

100

So every dark and stormy night—
the kind that shakes a house with fright—
if you stood still and listened right,

you'd hear a

teeny

tiny

BOO!

I HAD A DREAM LAST NIGHT
by Gwendolyn Brooks

I had a dream last night. I dreamed

I had to pick a mother out.

I had to choose a father too.

At first, I wondered what to do,

There were so many there, it seemed,

Short and tall and thin and stout.

But just before I sprang awake,
I knew what parents I would take.

And this surprised and made me glad:
They were the ones I already had!

DRIVING TO THE BEACH
by Joanna Cole

On the road
smell fumes and tar
through the windows
of the car.

But at the beach
smell suntan lotion
and wind
and sun
and ocean!

AT THE SEA-SIDE
by Robert Louis Stevenson

When I was down beside the sea

A wooden spade they gave to me

To dig the sandy shore.

My holes were empty like a cup.

In every hole the sea came up,

Till it could come no more.

THIS IS MY ROCK
by David McCord

This is my rock

And here I run

To steal the secret of the sun;

This is my rock

And here come I

Before the night has swept the sky;

This is my rock,

This is the place

I meet the evening face to face.

Fun and Games

*By Joanna Cole and
Stephanie Calmenson
Illustrated by Chris Demarest*

What is black and white

and red all over?

A sunburned zebra.

Why did the elephant

put on green shoes?

To hide in the grass.

110

What letter is found in a cup?

T.

What letter is an insect?

B.

What letter is part of your head?

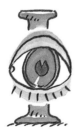

I.

How does a monster count to sixteen?

On its

fingers.

When are cooks mean?

When

they

beat the

eggs

and

whip

the

cream.

What is yellow, has feathers,

and pops up and down?

A canary

with

the hiccups.

I have teeth, but no mouth.

What am I?

A comb.

I have hands and a face,

but I can't touch or smile.

What am I?

A clock.

I have legs, but can't walk.

What am I?

A table.

I have eyes, but can't see.

What am I?

A potato.

Knock-knock.

Who's there?

Telly.

Telly who?

Telly-phone

is ringing.

Knock-knock.

Who's there?

You.

You who?

Yoo hoo,

to you too.

Knock-knock.

Who's there?

Annie.

Annie who?

Annie-body

see my hat?

119

What do you call a cat
who eats a lemon?

A sourpuss.

What do you call a fish
that chases mice?

A catfish.

What do you call a dog

at the beach?

A hot-dog.

"Hurry, hurry!" said the .

"It is going to !"

But her  did not hurry.

The  sniffed a .

The dog chased a .

122

The dog looked behind a 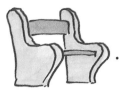.

"Run, run!" said the .

"The is coming!"

But her did not run.

The looked under a .

"Woof! Woof!" said the .

What did he find?

It was an .

"Good !"

said the 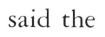.

Fran fried five flat fish.

Bill built blue bridges with big blocks.

Sue saw sheep in shoes.

Trudy tried three free things.

Wendy went to rent one red room.

Gwen grabbed green glue.

Dan's dad danced bad.

A baked a in her .

The was too hot.

The  put the  in the

to cool. The  went to

 to take a nap.

A  came to the 🏠. The saw the 🎂. The said, "Beep-beep-beep."

Do U know what that means?

It means, "👁 like 🎂!"

The 🦁 woke up.

The ⭕ was M-T!

What happened?

Do U know?

129

A pig in a wig do the jig?

A goat in a coat go in a boat?

Mice on ice? Don't they look nice?

A cat with a bat in a big red hat?

A frog on a log in a fog?

An egg on a wall catch a ball,

and then

fall?

One day a went -ing in a

little . But he did not get

any . "I have bad luck **2**-day,"

said the . A big  came up.

The  went in-**2**

the 's .

134

The  was scared. What bad luck!

But inside, there were lots of !

The  went

-ing.

Then the  swam to .

The got out.

"I had good luck

-day," he said.

apple balloon cat dog egg foot guita

ICE CREAM

GROCERIES

OPEN

WISE OWL
BOOKSTORE

nail owl pickle queen raccoon sock tr

ice cream jack-in-the-box kite leaf mouse

brella Valentine water X-ray yo-yo zipper

The rang at 's .

"Hello," said .

"Hello," said .

"Come to my .

  play with my ."

"No, thank you," said . "Come

to my . play with my ."

"It is better at my ," said .

"My mom just made ."

"My dad made ," said .

" have a new 📘," said 🐵.

"It is about 🦕."

" have a new 📘 2," said 🐰.

"It is about 🦈."

"My 📘 is better," said 🐵.

"It is 🪢," said 🐰.

"It is 2," said 🐵.

"Is 🪢!" said 🐰.

"Is 2!" said 🐵.

"👁 do 🐑 want 2 go 2 your 🏠," said 🐰.

"👁 do 🐑 want 2 go 2 your 🏠," said 🐵.

🐰 and 🐵 hung up their ☎☎.

🐵 was sad. 🐰 was sad 2.

🐵 got a 🛍. He put his 🚚 and his 📕 and some 🍌-🍞 in the 🛍.

He started 2 walk 2 🐰's 🏠. 🐰 got a 🛍. He put his ⛵ and his 📕

and some  in the .

He started 2 walk

2 's .

On the way, saw .

" was going 2 your

," said .

" was going 2 your ," said .

"We play right here," said

"Good idea!" said

and had a

wonderful time together.

TITLE INDEX

At the Sea-Side	105
Baby Chick	88
Come to My House	138
Did You Ever See…?	130
Driving to the Beach	104
Eating Worms	99
Fat Cat, The	84
Find the Hidden Pictures	136
Frog and Toad: Ice Cream	38
Giggle Poem	91
Hello, Hello	86
Hurry! Hurry!	122
I Had a Dream Last Night	102
I Left My Head	94
I Like Cake!	128
I Liked Growing	96
I Wouldn't	92
Morris Has a Cold	66
Notice	85
Our Earth in Space	50
Riddles	110
Seven Sillies in a Row	90
Sheep in a Jeep	12
Soft-Boiled Egg	98
Teeny Tiny Ghost	100
This Is My Rock	106
Tongue-Twisters	124
Whale Tale, A	134
What Will Little Bear Wear?	27

AUTHOR AND ARTIST INDEX

APPLE, MARGOT 12–26

BROOKS, GWENDOLYN 102–103

BURGESS, ANNE 83–107

CALMENSON, STEPHANIE 84, 90, 91
110–141

CIARDI, JOHN 92–93

COLE, JOANNA 50–65, 104
110–141

DEMAREST, CHRIS 1, 3, 7–9
109–141

FISHER, AILEEN 88–89

HOBAN, RUSSELL 98

KUSKIN, KARLA 96

LOBEL, ARNOLD 38–49

MAESTRO, GIULIO 50–65

McCORD, DAVID 85, 106

MERRIAM, EVE 86–87

MINARIK, ELSE HOLMELUND 27–37

MOORE, LILIAN 94, 100–101

SENDAK, MAURICE 27–37

SHAW, NANCY 12–26

STEVENSON, ROBERT LOUIS 105

WISEMAN, BERNARD 66–82

JOANNA COLE

has taught elementary school, has worked for a news magazine, and for several years was a senior editor for children's books. Today she is a full time author, writing for and about children. She has written dozens of books, including *Best-Loved Folktales of the World, A New Treasury of Children's Poetry,* and the popular "Magic School Bus" series. She lives in Connecticut, with her husband and daughter.

STEPHANIE CALMENSON,

also a former teacher, and author of many books for children, has been the editorial director of Parent's Magazine's Read-Aloud Book Club. Her books include *The Children's Aesop, Fido, What Am I?: Very First Riddles, Wanted: Warm, Furry Friend,* and *The Principal's New Clothes.* She grew up in Brooklyn and lives in Manhattan.

Together, Joanna Cole and Stephanie Calmenson have written *Safe from the Start: Your Child's Safety from Birth to Age Five,* and have compiled three other anthologies for children, *The Laugh Book, The Scary Book,* and *The Read-Aloud Treasury.*